We Can Cook!

by Abbie Rushton

illustrated by Emily Cooksey

OXFORD
UNIVERSITY PRESS

Aiden has a cookbook.

Can we cook
a quick dish?

Yes!

Quick Fish Dish

You will need ...

fish

leeks

carrots

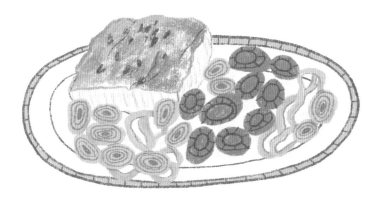

1. Cook the chips.

Dad peels.

He chops the
chips into chunks.

Aiden coats the thick chips.

He puts them in the tin.

The chips go in to cook.

I can not wait!

2. Cook the fish.

Aiden dips the fish in egg.

We need to coat the fish.

Look at my foot! It is a mess!

9

Aiden coats the fish.

It coats me!

Dad cooks the fish in a pan.

3. Cook the leeks and carrots.

Dad chops the leeks and carrots.

Aiden puts them in a pan.
The leeks and carrots cook.

Dad gets the chip tin.
He puts it on a wooden mat.

15

Cook the chips

1. _____
2. chop
3. coat

Cook the fish

1. dip
2. _____

Cook the leeks and carrots

1. peel
2. _____

chop   coat   peel